ANIMALS AND THEIR BABIES

Frogs and Tadpoles

written by Anita Ganeri

illustrated by Anni Axworthy

CHERRYTREE BOOKS

A Cherrytree book

Published by
Evans Publishing Group
2A Portman Mansions
Chiltern St
London W1U 6NR

First published in 2007

Printed in China by WKT Co Ltd

British Library Cataloguing in Publication Data
Ganeri, Anita, 1961-
    Frogs and tadpoles. - (Animals and their babies)
    1. Tadpoles - Juvenile literature 2. Frogs - Life cycles -
    Juvenile literature
    I. Title
    597.8'9156

ISBN 978184 234439 2

CONTENTS

A frog starts life as a tiny egg.
In springtime, a female frog lays the eggs in a pond. The eggs are called frogspawn.

The female lays hundreds of eggs at a time, but some of them are eaten by other frogs, and birds.
The eggs look like little blobs of jelly, each with a tiny black dot inside. The eggs stick together in a big wobbly ball.

What are the black dots inside the blobs of jelly? Each dot is a tiny tadpole. Inside the eggs, the tadpoles grow bigger and bigger.

After about a month, the eggs start to hatch.

A squirming tadpole wriggles out of its
jelly ball. This tiny tadpole will grow into
a baby frog.

But the tadpole doesn't look like a frog yet.
It has a long, wiggly tail like a fish. It uses
its tail for swimming about in the pond.

Every day, the tiny tadpole grows bigger and stronger. It feeds on plants growing in the water. It scrapes off pieces of the plants to eat.

When the tadpole
is six weeks old, it
grows two legs at the back.

Four weeks later, it grows
two legs at the front.

The tadpole still uses its
tail for swimming. But now it uses
its webbed feet as flippers as well.

The tadpole's tail grows shorter and shorter until it's almost gone. At 12 weeks old, it doesn't look like a fish any more. It looks like a little frog!

The little frog is four months old. It climbs out of the water. It hops on to a plant stem growing by the waterside.

On land, the frog likes damp, dark places best. During the day, it hides away from animals that might gobble it up.

Animals such as birds, bats and snakes like frogs to eat. When the frog is in danger, it dives back into the pond. Splosh!

When the frog is hungry, it sits very still
and waits. Then it pokes out its long, sticky
tongue and gobbles the insect up!

A juicy worm makes another tasty treat
for the frog. It's gone in one big gulp.

When it is three years old, the frog is grown up. It goes back to the pond it was born in. There, the male and female frogs mate. Then the female frog lays her eggs in the water.

Soon the eggs will turn into tiny tadpoles.
And the tadpoles will turn into...

...lots of new little frogs!

Index

Further Information

The frogs featured in this book are common frogs (*Rana temporaria*). To find out more about them, you can visit: www.bbc.co.uk/nature/wildfacts/factfiles